This Book
Belongs To:

_____

_____

_____

Recipes Sworn to Secrecy [TM]

Michaelis Publishing Corp.
2274 South 1300 East #G8-288
Salt Lake City, Utah 84106

Library of Congress Catalog Card Number:
94-75229 Second Printing

Front Cover by Etola Zinni
Printed in the United States of America
1994

ISBN: 1-884084-08-7

Recipes Sworn To Secrecy

An International Collection of Family and Favorite Recipes.

By Constantina and Nikos Linardakis

Michaelis Publishing Corp.
Athens   Chicago   Salt Lake City
Singapore   Burr Ridge

Dedication

This book is dedicated with admiration to the families who preserve their love in the food they create and to sharing the recipes with us for this special book.

Secrets In Order of Presentation

∞

Introduction

This irresistible and appetizing cookbook of some thirty unique recipes has been written for people desiring more in a cookbook. This book provides the "keys" to unlock several kitchen doors for their secrets. Prior to each creative recipe is the unique and entertaining story of its origin. The collection of recipes are introduced with thought-provoking quotations to enhance the book's character and artistic display. We know you will find the quotes and the stories of *Recipes Sworn to Secrecy* fulfilling to read.

In writing this book, several details were communicated between the editors, publisher, and contributors. The objectives and guidelines required from the beginning to the end of the book were obsessively followed. After nearly two years of continued correspondence between contributors, we have completed *Recipes Sworn to Secrecy*. We appreciate the encouragement from both of our mothers as we reinvented the traditional cookbook into a modern-day recipe book. A special toast to all of the contributors who generously offered helpful hints, tips and stories with their recipes. We also thank Claude Guigon of Sun Valley, Idaho, and other chefs from across the globe for their comments. Special congratulations to all who were a part of this long project. Although several submitted recipes were not included in this volume of *Recipes Sworn to Secrecy*, we may include them in a future volume.

Along with the original creators, we invite you to our table for a rare dining experience as we proudly introduce the following *Recipes Sworn to Secrecy*.

Constantina & Nikos Linardakis

"When you really care about something, you get involved."

—Nikos Linardakis

"Secrets are things we give to others to keep for us."

—Elbert Hubbard

Appetizers

If you are an adventurous, frugal or eclectic cook, then this recipe is for you. It evolved from a combination of events in our first year of marriage as I experimented in the kitchen of my little apartment in Chicago. Along with my successes there were a few failures. The only good thing about failures is that we got to go out for dinner. One of these nights my husband and I went to an Indian restaurant and were pleasently surprised with the new flavors and scents the Indian cuisine had to offer. "Hmmm, I have to incorporate this into my cooking", I thought.

Being of Greek descent, I enjoy the taste of hot, crisp filo (phyllo) dough stuffed with an array of goodies ranging from cheese to meats to sweet creams. The Greeks however never ventured as far as I have with versatility of this delicate dough. It's a little tricky to work with, but if bought frozen and SLOWLY thawed as per direction on the box, one should be able to easily peel each thin sheet with ease and wrap up your filling beautifully.

This recipe is simply an outline for you to experiment with and alter to your taste. It's frugal because most any veggie will do. Just open up that crisper and lets get cooking!

Antigone Polite

Antigone's Wrap-Ups

1. Boil 3 cups of water in a large pot. Add lentils.
2. Return to boil for 45 minutes on medium-low heat. Stir occasionally checking the consistency of the lentils. Add water as it absorbed. The lentils should be soft and mushy.
3. Toss the vegetables into the pot of lentils and stir well.   Cook over low heat until all the vegetables are soft. (About 30 min.) Stir occasionally and add water to keep it from getting too thick. At this point it is optional to puree the mixture if you prefer a smooth filling or don't puree if you would like a chunkier one. Stop cooking when it is the consistency of applesauce. Allow to cool and thicken.
4. Using the suggestion on the filo box, cut the filo in strips and only work with a few pieces at a time. Keep the remaining filo under a moist towel to avoid cracking. Lightly brush the strip of filo with butter. Use about 1/2 teaspoonful of filling and fold into triangles (like you used to make paper footballs when you were a kid).
5. Put them on a cookie sheet evenly spaced 1/2" or more apart (this allows for even browning on sides). Bake at 350 degrees for 20-25 minutes. They should be golden brown.

Base Filling
1 cup red,yellow, or brown lentils in any proportion-rinsed
4-6 cups of water

Add-ins
1 tsp. curry powder
1/4 tsp. coriander
3 tbsp. tomato paste
1/3 cup chopped onion
1 clove of garlic-minced

2 cups of any vegetables i.e. carrots, celery, eggplant, tomato, zucchini, potatoes

1 package of filo dough
1 cup melted butter
1 pastry brush

Violet flowers lined the surroundings of a Sedona, Phoenix coffee shop and restaurant. The pleasant views from the entrance of the restaurant enlightened this recipe. As I was experimenting for a sorbet recipe in Burr Ridge, I turned towards the properties of this flower. The creme of the romantic violet flower is a secret ingredient for the sorbet.

Constantina Linardakis

Violet Sorbet

1. Mix lime juice, grape juice, sugar syrup, creme de violette.

2. Freeze until soft and mushy.

3. Take out of freezer then add the egg white and fold in caster sugar. Refreeze (about 1 hour). Serve in glasses and decorate with violets.

2 tbsp. lime juice
1/2 pt. grape juice
1/3 pt. sugar syrup
4 tbsp. Creme De Violette

2 oz. caster sugar
1 egg white

Special Ingredients/Tips

Creme de Violette is a product of France and can be purchased at a specialty liquor store.

"An empty stomach is not a good political advisor."

—Albert Einstein

  *Vegetables*

Vegetables

Smith Family
Brownsville, Texas

As a new wife living in Brownsville, Texas, I was making a basic recipe for pinto beans in my crock pot. My neighbor, a hispanic native Texan happened to be over and suggested I add a few extra ingredients to my beans. Over the years I've perfected the beans and they get a "thumbs up" from all those who like their beans very hot. I've never been able to get a clear translation for the Spanish word, "charro" but I think a good one might be..."heat sufficient for one to break into a sweat". Here's my secret recipe...

Rhonda Smith

Charro Beans

1. Rinse 1 lb. pinto beans in colander
2. Place in crock pot with:
     1 chopped onion
     4 chopped bacon strips
     5 small servano peppers, diced
     1/2 bunch of fresh cilantro, diced
     1-2 teaspoons salt
3. Fill crock pot with water till 1 inch from top.
4. Cook on low overnight and into the next afternoon.
Stir occasionally and test beans for tenderness.
Serve in individual cups (like soup).
Great with fajitas!

1 lb. pinto beans
1 chopped onion
4 chopped bacon strips
5 small servano peppers
(diced)
1/2 bunch of fresh
cilantro, (diced)
1-2 teaspoons salt

Special Ingredients/Tips

- Cilantro, fresh, sometimes called coriander

- Serrano peppers are smaller than jalepenos and hotter.

Akan Family
Casablanca, Morocco

"You will very much like this dish...The recipe was kept in my desk for years and remained a secret until now. This is for my favorite friends."

Joesph Akan

Couscous Moroccan Style

1. Combine couscous and currants. Pour boiling broth over. Mix. Let stand for 5 minutes.

2. Combine chick peas and tomatoes (chick peas drained) in a separate pan cook for five minutes on medium heat.

3. Add peas, cumin, salt and cayenne pepper. Mix well. Add salt and cayenne pepper to taste to couscous. Sprinkle with fresh cilantro.

1 cup instant couscous
1/3 cup dried currants
2/3 cup broth
1 can (16 ounces) chick peas.
1 can diced tomatoes
1/2 cup peas
1/2 teaspoon cumin
cayenne pepper
1-2 teaspoons salt & pepper.

Special Ingredients/Tips

- Chicken Broth works best with this recipe.

"The secret of success is consistency of purpose."

—Benjamin Disraeli

Soups & Chili

Bates Family
Coalville, Utah

My German grandma made the best chili. She used hamburger and beans in her chili. Many times her recipes changed because the ingredients she needed were not available or she did not have the money to buy them. What I learned from her is to improvise.

This recipe evolved with a little German, a little Spanish, a little pioneer Mormon, and a lot of country. I entered this in a chili contest held in Salt Lake City, Utah and won a cash prize and ribbon. It was cooked outside in a large iron deep pan. I think you will enjoy this chili and here is my secret recipe.

Christine Bates

Country Chili

1. Brown 1lb. stew meat. Set aside.

2. Saute in bacon grease or butter, onions, green pepper, red pepper, and 1 clove of garlic.

3. Combine meat and peppers, onions, and garlic into a large pot. Set aside.

4. Add 16 ounces stewed tomatoes, sugar, oregano and bay leaves. Add salt and pepper to taste. Simmer for 45 minutes.

5. Add 2 cans kidney beans with liquid. Continue to cook until meat is tender and flavor of spices is all through the chili. Add chili powder the last 15 minutes of cooking. For a hotter chili, add a little tabasco sauce. Chili tastes better after sitting in refrigerator overnight.

6. Serve with cornbread. Add mild cheddar cheese over top and Fritos® or corn chips.

1 lb. stew meat
2 chopped onions
1 chopped green pepper
1 chopped red pepper
1 clove garlic
16 ounces stewed tomatoes(Italian style)
2 tablespoons sugar
1 teaspoon salt
1 teaspoon pepper
oregano to taste
bay leaves to taste
2 cans kidney beans with liquid.

Special Ingredients/Tips

- *If you prefer meatless, make this without bacon grease and no meat.*

Flavor is the gift of this special soup. A few extra ingredients have been added over the last few years. It is a fine blend of versatile flavors that are very healthy as well. On a cool evening, spoonfuls of the herb bisque will please the palate and warm the soul. The recipe originated in my family in Connecticut around 1850. It remained in my mother's cupboard and was rewritten by my aunts. Now, the recipe is as close to its original presentation. I thank my mother for her kind determination in reading the original recipe, and here it is...

June Kurt

Herb Bisque

1. In a large stockpot melt the butter over low heat.

2. Cook and stir the onion, celery, and carrot 4 minutes, until softened. Spread the flour over the vegetables and cook, continue to stir for 1 minute.

3. Add broth, garlic cloves, pepper, bay leaves, and tomatoes. Heat at high and boil. Decrease heat and simmer, uncovered for 1 1/2 hours. (Sometimes, butter and flour forms a layer on the surface, you can remove this.) After it thickens, pour liquid through a fine strainer (this removes more lumps).

4. Transfer the soup to a clean stockpot and boil over medium heat. Add whipping cream. Mix the pine nuts and olive oil in a skillet over medium heat. Cook and stir for 1 minute.

5. Place the pine nuts and olive oil in a blender, and add the minced garlic, cheese, basil, and 1/4 cup of soup. Blend until smooth. Add this to the bisque, and add salt.
It's now ready to serve!

1 celery stalk, chopped
1 carrot, chopped
1 onion, chopped
4 Tbsp. unsalted butter

1/4 cup grated
Parmesan cheese
Two 1/2 quarts
vegetable broth
3 tbsp. all-purpose flour
4 bay leaves
4 garlic cloves
1 tsp. black pepper

2 tomatoes (chopped)
1 cup whipping cream
4 tbsp pine nuts
1 tbsp. olive oil
2 tbsp. minced garlic
3 bunches fresh basil

Use your favorite vegetable broth recipe for broth mixture.

"Some painters transform the sun with a yellow spot, others transform a yellow spot into the sun."

—Pablo Picasso

Breakfast Foods

Breakfast Foods

This recipe was one that originated from Denmark by my Great Grandmother Hinderman. Her name was Signa. She came to America from Denmark when she was a beautiful 18 year old girl. This recipe seems similar to today's crepe, but there are a few additions to it with serving tips that make it unique. The best part to enjoying the pancakes is in the preparation of them before eating. They turn out thin and the size of a dinner plate. Anyone in the family for generations refers to them as "Big Pancakes". Indeed they are! As a child, my family marvelled at how many I could eat at one sitting for being such a little girl.

It is claimed that the best success is achieved when using an exclusive heavy cast iron pan (pan can only be used for this). Any time my own mother fails to make one of Signa's Big Pancakes on the first try, she swears it's because she made something earlier in the week using this iron pan. Then we hear about a big, old skillet she used to use (probably Grandma Hinderman's!) just for the pancake recipe, but cannot find it anywhere. (We suspect someone in the family "borrowed" it--the family "secret treasure" it must have been!) But it's still Mom who makes these pancakes the best!

The recipe seems easy enough by its ingredients, but it does become a little tricky when the large pancake is ready to be flipped over without breaking or folding it. Most important is to remain patient, persevere and strictly buy a heavy cast iron pan labelling it "TO BE USED FOR BIG PANCAKES ONLY!" ... and here is my secret recipe!

Etola Zinni

Signa's Big Pancakes

1. Place first three dry ingredients in a bowl adding enough milk to make a gravy. Add two eggs. Stir well. Add more milk until quite thin in consistency.

2. In heavy, black pan (cast iron), melt about one teaspoon of shortening to cover the bottom of the pan over a high flame. When heated, drop one ladle full of pancake batter into the pan lowering the flame a bit. Immediately move the pan around so the batter covers the bottom completely. Allow the batter to set up. It doesn't take long. Once set, shake the pan a bit to dislodge the pancake from the bottom. (They have a tendency to lightly stick in some spots.)

3. You will now be ready to gently turn the pancake over in the pan. Carefully, slide a large spatula underneath one end towards the middle. Flip it over quickly, trying not to let the pancake buckle upon falling. (It may take a few attempts to achieve a perfect pancake. Once you begin, they turn out better with every try.) Slide the lightly browned pancake onto a warm plate. It is ready to garnish with butter and brown sugar.

1 cup flour
2 tbsp. sugar
cinnamon - dash

Milk (whole or 2%)
2 eggs
1 tsp. shortening
butter
brown sugar

Serving Tip

You may stack the pancakes on a warm platter if making many at one time. To handle each pancake, thread one with the tines of fork, roll onto the fork and unroll onto your plate.

Lesowski Family
British Colombia, Canada

My parents lived on a farm in the mountains of British Columbia 20 miles from the nearest town. In the early 1930's they didn't go to town often, when they did they bought flour and sugar by the 100 pound bags.

My mother baked all her own bread. Often when she baked bread she would take some of the bread dough and make cinnamon rolls. Any one who ate these rolls raved of how good they were. My mother is now gone, but people are still talking about the cinnamon rolls and have never had any since, that were like hers. I know you'll enjoy our family's secret recipe...

Joan Lesowski

Cinnamon Rolls

1. Dissolve yeast in warm water with a pinch of sea salt. add the three dry ingredients - bread flour, baking powder, and sea salt - in a large bowl. Knead well.

2. Take the bread dough and roll rectangular to about 1/2 inch thick. Spread generously with thick cow's cream.

3. Sprinkle with 1 to 2 cups of white sugar. Shake cinnamon over this. Raisins nuts or coconuts can be added at this time. Roll like a jelly roll and cut in slices about 1 & 1/2 inches thick.

4. Put slices in greased pan leaving a little space to give them room to rise. The pan should have fairly high sides (2 inches or better). Let rise until double, bake at 350 degrees for 30 to 40 minutes. When done turn upside down on a plate, they don't need icing as the cream and sugar makes a nice candy topping.

1 package yeast
1 pinch sea salt
1 cup warm water
3 cups bread flour
1 large pinch of baking powder
1 teaspoon sea salt
2 tablespoons butter
Cow's Cream
1 - 2 cups white sugar
Cinnamon
Raisins
Nuts or Coconut

Special Ingredients/Tips

Substitute whipping cream if you cannot find cow's cream..

"There is no love sincerer than the love of food."

—George Bernard Shaw

Main Dishes

W. Family
Carlingford, Australia

This recipe has been a part of our family cookbook for many years. It was shared with us so long ago now, we have forgotten its origin and regard it as our own. We use the loaf regularly for weekend or holiday meals, either served on its own or with a salad. Its a special favorite of ours and would only release it to a cookbook, "Recipes Sworn to Secrecy".

L. W.

Salmon Seas Loaf

1. Combine flour and salt in a basin and rub margarine through it until soft and crumbly.

2. Combine together with sour cream or water. Chill for 1 1/2 hours (if possible). Roll out lightly on floured board till approximately 10" by 15". Put in dish.

3. Combine rice, salmon (undrained), parsley, onion, tomato paste, salt, pepper, lemon and 3/4 beaten egg.

4. Place mixture in center of pastry (in dish). Fold sides in and glaze lightly with rest of beaten egg. Slash diagonally on top, or leave spaces in pastry on top. Bake at 425 degrees for 25 - 30 minutes. Serve hot.

2 cups flour
3/4 tsp. salt

4 oz. margarine
1 cup sour cream
or 2/3 cup water

1 cup cooked rice
(1/3 cup uncooked rice)
1 large tine of Salmon
(or tuna)
1 can of tomato paste
1 onion finely chopped
or onion flakes
1 tbsp. chopped parsley
salt, pepper, squeeze
of lemon
1 egg

Klimala Family
Oak Brook, Illinois

*W*hile lying in bed one night, I had a dream. I was head chef at Jeff's Chop Suey and Steak House and operated a small laundromat. I always wanted to own a laundromat and run a restaurant business. I decided in my dream that I was tired of the same chinese and bland steak house food. So I came up with my " A- 1" stir fry. When I woke up I went straight to the supermarket and bought all the ingredients. It turned out perfect! I still don't own my laundromat though.

Jeff Klimala

Jeff's Downtown "A-1" Stir Fry

1. Cut chicken into 3/4" chunks and marinate in a mixture of soy, worcestershire, tabasco and ginger sauces for 1/2 hour.

2. Start cooking the rice (45 minutes cooking time), while rice cooks and chicken marinates, chop and slice all vegetables to your own taste.

3. With 15 minutes left on the rice, fry the vegetables, water chestnuts, and bamboo shoots in 2 tablespoons of rice bran or olive oil. Taint with ginger and stir fry sauce.

4. When hot & slightly browned take out vegetables & cover in a separate bowl. Start to fry the chicken in same amount of oil. While frying add vegetables after 5 - 10 minutes and stir in 2 tablespoons peanut sauce, 2 tablespoons A-1 sauce®, and 2 tablespoons stir fry sauce. When all items are sufficiently cooked and mixed together, lay on a bed of brown rice. Add soy sauce to rice to your liking before adding stir fry.

1 lb. boneless chicken
1 cup brown rice
ginger spice
handful of water chestnuts
handful of bamboo shoots
1/4 cucumber sliced thin
1 large broccoli crown
2 carrots
1 onion 1 red pepper
1 green pepper
10 -12 peapods
1 tsp. tabasco sauce
1 tsp. soy sauce
1 tsp. peanut (thai) sauce
2 tsps. A-1 sauce®
stir fry sauce
worcestershire sauce
rice bran or olive oil

It was a cool spring night when the realization finally hit me that I would be soon be leaving home...this time for real. Sure, I had spent 4 years aways in college, but never had I strayed so far away as to be outside of driving range from my mom's home cooking. I'm not a fancy eater, mind you. It's just that there are some culinary needs that can not be met by soon to be best friends Oscar Meyer and M.C. Donalds.

The solution seemed simple, I would simply ask my mom to teach me how to make it on my own. After all, I was an accomplished chemist heading off to seek my fortune of knowledge in chemistry graduate school. How difficult could it be to prepare? To my surprise, the preparation was to be the least of my problems. It was the acquisition of the recipe which proved to be difficult!

So I set off to spend the day learning from the master. Here is an amazing 70 year old woman from the old country who talks about how simple life is here in America where she does not have to grind the wheat to make the flour needed for her daily bread baking routine. You get the picture that this is a self sufficient woman....and a great cook. What follows is the first written version of a recipe which has been handed down from generation to generation of Greek women (and now men) since Plato was a kid.

Lee Polite

Andromachi's Pastitsio

Brown 1 pound of lean ground beef with onion. Add salt and pepper to taste. Add one tablespoon of ground cinnamon. Add tomato paste and mix thoroughly. Under low heat, add two egg whites to the ground beef and stir continuously. Allow to heat for a few minutes with stirring. Set this aside until later. Prepare Macaroni and Cheese per package instruction. Set this aside. Lightly grease a casserole pan 9x12 with Crisco® and then add bread crumbs until there is a light coating of cracker meal over the whole pan. Add the macaroni and cheese to the pan and spread evenly. Now add the ground beef on top of the macaroni and spread evenly. Make sure that there is still at least 1 to 1.5 inches of room on the top of the ground beef. Set aside. Heat whole milk and half/half to a near boil and keep hot until later. Place 2 whole eggs and the remaining 2 yolks into a blender with the parmesan cheese. Mix on high speed and set aside until later. In a separate pan, prepare a roux by heating one stick of butter until it begins to turn brown and then add flour. When this mixture turns to a reddish-brown smooth paste, add the heated milk, stir well for 2 minutes and add egg mixture. It is important to stir this mixture over light heat until it thickens to a consistency of runny oatmeal. At that point, pour the "crema" over the ground beef. Place the casserole into a preheated oven at 375 degrees for 45 minutes.

1 pound of lean ground beef.
1 small onion
1 tbsp. cinnamon
6 ounces tomato paste
4 eggs
1 package Kraft ®
Macaroni and Cheese
(deluxe)
Crisco®
bread crumbs
1 quart whole milk
1 pint half-n-half
1/8 parmesan cheese
1/4 cup sifted all
purpose flour

"Wow! What's in this pizza?" Guests ask as they crave another piece. My generous slices are actually a layered creation that originated in Chicago. The pizza was initially made for my beautiful wife (she is originally from Salt Lake City, and never tried *real* Chicago-style pizza). I was born and raised in the Chicago area in a large Greek family. We had very good family cooks (my mother and her sisters were always in the kitchen) who baked and prepared all the tastes of the world. I had particularly grown a "taste" for a special pizzeria in the Chicago area which bears my wife's name. I must admit this recipe is an original, but it was inspired by the flavor of the local pizzeria. I was even ready to work long hours in the kitchen to find their secret. I finally produced this unique pizza and labeled it as my own. I will share the secret here as a unique combination of the flavor from an imported beer like Heineken®, which is used to marinate the butcher's finest Italian sausage. All of the ingredients should be of top quality. It is a delicious pizza and is guaranteed to make you full. The cheese is a sumptuous blend of flavors, and it is necessary to add the entire amount (the cheese should be very thick). The pizza was created in a Chicago oven which may add another flavor; try a pizza stone for your oven.

Nikos Linardakis

Niko's Chicago Deep-dish Pizza

1. Prepare salsa mixture. Set aside.

2. In a large bowl, dissolve yeast in water. Stir in sugar, salt and olive oil. Add 1 cup flour and beat until smooth. Mix in remaining flour until dough forms. Cover; let rise in warm place about 20 minutes. Turn out onto lightly floured surface, knead 8 minutes.

3. Cook marinated sausage at 425 degrees for 20 minutes.

4. Grease heavy 16 inch metal round pizza tray. Sprinkle lightly with cornmeal. Roll dough out 1/2 inch larger than pan; press into bottom and up sides. Leave a thick side for crust.

5. With oven at 425 degrees. Top pizza dough with salsa. Arrange generous amounts of sausage onto the salsa. Layer with cheese. Bake 25 minutes or until cheese is melted and crust is lightly browned. Cut into 6 to 8 large pie shaped slices.

Prepare 1 lb. mild sausage by marinating overnight in 6 oz. of imported beer, oregano, and lemon juice.

Pizza Crust Dough
1 pkg. active dry yeast
3 cups flour
1 tsp. sugar
1/2 tsp. salt
1 cup warm water
1 tbsp. olive oil
cornmeal

Cheese Blend
2 cups mozzarella,
1 cup smoked romano
1 cup provolone

Salsa Mixture
1 clove garlic
sliced mushrooms
2 cups tomato sauce
2 tsp. oregano
1 tbsp. olive oil
fresh basil
1 tsp. black pepper
2 tsp. red wine
1/2 tsp. salt

The recipe I'm about to present has been in my family since 1870, at which time it was handed down through my grandparent's French lineage.

As a young girl born and raised in Yugoslavia, I learned to observe my mother prepare this dish. In Yugoslavia, it is very common to prepare meals for large groups of people since once the males married it was understood they would stay with their wife and family in the same home as their parents. So my brothers and their wives and children all lived with me until I too married. Roladen is not very complex to make. I have even won an award in the *Los Angeles Magazine* for its presentation. You'll enjoy my secret recipe.

Angie Burdick

Roladen

1. Mix stuffing ingredients. Set aside.

2. Prepare slices for stuffing by laying each out flat and place about 1/2 cup stuffing on each. Top with 1/2 slice raw bacon, smoked. Add 1/2 strip dill pickle slice.

3. Roll-up, tucking ends, securing with wooden skewers. Take extra large frying pan or electric skillet. Use 1/4 cup olive oil to brown Roladen, heating oil first before adding meat. Brown all sides.

4. Take 1/2 lb. regular butter (2 cubes) & add to meat in skillet. Add 1 cup boiling water, 1 cup dry red wine.

5. Sprinkle pepper and rosemary over meat. Take 2 tbsp. flour, mixed well with 1/4 cup water & pour around sides of pan. Bring to boil & lower heat to simmer, cooking for 1 hour, stirring frequently. Add 2 cups fresh mushrooms added 15 minutes before done (after 45 minutes cooking).

Stuffing
1 box Stuffing crumbs
1 meduim onion
2 cloves garlic
2 Tbsp. fresh parsley
1/2 tsp. blackpepper
1 can beef consumme
1 egg

Roladen
12 slices, 1/4 " thick
top sirloin from roast.
Spread each slice with
A-1 sauce® .
3 Dill pickles
1 pkg. bacon
1/4 cup olive oil
2 cubes butter
1 cup dry red wine
2 tbsp. flour
one & 1/2 tsp. rosemary
2 cups fresh mushrooms
1/2 tsp. pepper

Special Ingredients/Tips

- Have butcher slice top sirloin for you into 1/4" strips from Roast.

"I had been laid off from my job and was experiencing an uneventful job position search. How was I to bring dinner for my family? The only items were pasta and such. It was this delicious recipe that created the family meal and stirred my energy to help my job search. It eventually became my most delightful meal years later." These were the approximate words of my father, who to this day still enjoys my designer macaroni and cheese recipe, it is wonderful how he returned to his job and advanced to have a successful career.

James Sullivan

Designer Macaroni and Cheese

1. Peel potatoes and cut into 1/4 inch squares. Place in cold water.

2. Bring a large pot of salted water to a boil on stove, add macaroni, and cook 5 minutes. Drain potatoes and add to the macaroni. Cook 1 minute. Drain and add 2 tablespoons of olive oil (to prevent from sticking). Preheat oven to 375 degrees.

3. Take remaining olive oil and pine nuts in a meduim skillet or saucepan and cook over medium heat, about 3 minutes.

4. Add the garlic and cream, heat to a boil, and continue boiling until the cream and olive oil combine, about 1 minute.

5. Add the cream mixture, milk, and half of each cheese to macaroni and potatoes. Mix. Place in a 9 - inch by 13-inch baking dish and spinkle with the remaining cheese. Place in oven, uncovered for 20 minutes.

1/4 pd. raclette cheese (grated)
1/4 pd. Gruyere cheese (grated)
1/2 pd. russet potatoes
1/2 pd. uncooked elbow macroni
6 tbsp. virgin olive oil
1/4 cup pine nuts
2 tbsp. minced garlic
1 cup whipping cream
1 cup milk

Special Ingredients/Tips

- Raclette and Gruyere cheese can be purchased at delicatessan
- Makes a good buffet item.

This magical poultry dish came into the kitchen of 2 brothers by a little boy whose grandmother wanted to cook dinner for the local town. Each morning the boy delightfully travelled two blocks to come to the owners of the restaurant, and told them to allow his grandmother her wish to please everyone. The owner, who was in love with the boy's sister, was enchanted with the idea and offered the woman his restaurant for the evening. That night, a dinner was set with a sherry blend to toast the meeting of this couple. This recipe has been passed from one family to the next (two blocks down each time) with the hope that people will always remember their loved ones and those who they care about, both living and passed away.

Paul Martinez

Arroz con Pollo

1. Place chicken in seasoned flour.

2. In a large frying pan: heat oil and add garlic, onion, and chicken.
Cook chicken until brown.

3. Add tomatoes, parsley, peppers, and seasonings.

4. Pour chicken stock and simmer. Stir in rice and gently simmer for 45 minutes.

5. Pour sherry over chicken and rice, if desired.

Seasoned Flour Mixture:
1 cup flour
1 teaspoon salt
1/2 teaspoon paprika
1/2 teaspoon pepper
Sift all ingredients.

2 1/2 pounds chicken fryers, cut
3 cups chicken stock
1 &1/2 cups seasoned flour
1/2 cup olive oil
2 cloves minced garlic
1/2 cup chopped onion.
5 fresh tomatoes, diced
1 green pepper, sliced
1 sweet red pepper, sliced
1/2 cup chopped parsley
1 bay leaf
1/4 teaspoon saffron
1 1/2 tsp. seasoned salt
2 cups uncooked long grain rice.
1/2 cup sherry

Using my culinary techniques, this recipe may be different from others who try to match it, but I have placed within the ingredients and presentation the exact recipe minus the flare that comes with every chef. I am sure that you will have this unique talent and will enchant your guests with that part of the recipe that can only be created by you. Together, with many of my favorite additions, this simple dish will soon become one of your favorites.

Inocencio Esparza

Poulet Basque Style

1. Salt and pepper the chicken and set aside. Over a grill or direct flame, char pepper skins until black.

2. Wrap peppers in a damp paper towel for 5 minutes. Peel away burnt skins and cut peppers into thin strips.

Garnish
3. Place 3 tbsp. of olive oil in a large saute pan. Add onions and cook over medium heat until translucent. Add pepper strips, tomatoes with juice and garlic. Season with salt and pepper.

4. Stir to mix thoroughly and set aside. In a large saute pan over medium high heat, heat remaining olive oil, add chicken and brown on both sides until golden.

5. Remove chicken from pan and discard fat. Add vegetables to pan and place chicken on top, cover and cook over medium heat 25 to 30 minutes, turning once. To serve, spoon vegetables onto a warm platter and place chicken on top.

one 4 pound chicken quartered
2 green bell peppers
1 red bell pepper
1/3 cup olive oil
2 large onions, sliced
1 cup canned tomatoes with juice
4 cloves garlic, minced
salt and pepper, to taste

vegetables of choice

"What in God's name made you decide to cook fish!" Proclaimed my unwilling husband. It was a day that had to be considered as triumphant as the invention of the wheel. This dish is prepared to capture any person who has the fond taste for salmon, and will surely make the dinner one to remember. I have created Salmon a la Noire for my most loving and critical partner. It presents with a delightful taste that will be desired long after the dinner is finished. For the flavor, for the health, and for the smile that will be remembered and desired for in the next dinner, luxuriate in my secret recipe!

Aldi Von Wolf

Salmon A la Noire

1. Prepare fish fume set aside.

2. Place salmon fillets, fish fume, thyme, white wine and juice of lemon in a large skillet, bring to low simmer.

3. Once simmering let salmon cook for 4-5 minutes, and then turn over fillets. After turning over fillets and yellow squash, zucchini, potatoes, green beans, carrot flowers, and juliene onion to the fume. Cover skillet and allow to simmer for 3-4 minutes or until vegetables are soft.

4. Place salmon in a large soup bowl, arrange vegetable garnish around fillet and top off bowl with fume.

Serve immediately.

four 7 oz. salmon fillets
4 cups fish fume
8 tournee yellow squash
8 tournee zucchini
8 tournee potatoes
4 oz. French green beans
16 pc. carrot flowers
1 red onion
1 fresh thyme bunch
2 oz. white wine
1 lemon

Fume Broth
3 stalks celery
3 leeks
2 small onions
4 cups water
cook fish for 1 hour

Special Ingredients/Tips

Utilize an additional salmon or any other fish for fume.

"Novelty is the great parent of pleasure."

—Robert South

"Hunger is the best sauce."

—Proverb

Sauces

I prepared this sauce at an evening dinner with the most handsome man that I have ever met. It is interesting that I always talk of this man who came into my heart in 1941, and we spent an entire week together, only to find that he had to go back to the United States. After 2 years of writing, we met again and rekindled the fire. Of course I prepared the identical dish that was my secret recipe created with my mother and all of my heart. It is an enlightening recipe that should fill your hearts as well. And yes, even several children later, Thomas has been as darling as the day we met...

Margarita Follio

Argentine Chimichurri Sauce

Meat
Season beef or lamb and roast to desired state.

Sauce
Mix all ingredients together in a bottle or jar. Let stand for at least 12 hours, preferably a full day. Shake prior to use. Change spices according to personal taste.

Meat
Choose meat of choice typically beef works best.

Sauce
1/2 cup oil
1 cup vinegar
1 tsp. salt
2 cloves crushed garlic
2 tbsp. finely chopped parsley
1 scallion, chopped
1 small tomato, chopped
1 small sweet pepper
1/2 tsp. cumin
1/2 tsp. paprika
1/2 tsp. chili powder
2 bay leaves
1/2 tsp. oregano

Chef Richard Castleberry
Boca Raton, Florida

Flavor and color for a dish have always been an important part of a cook's presentation. Even a dessert with a smooth topping, elegantly displayed in patterns unique to the chef, may transform the once simple to an ever elaborate dish that shows the time and effort exerted by the chef. The Tahini dressing presented herein has become an established favorite addition to vegetable dishes, and creative covering for several meat creations. Remember, the dressing is pleasing to taste and color for a dish; as an interior decorator would decorate a home, your task is to "decorate" the dish by placing the dressing in a scheme that will be remembered by the patron. After you have chosen a pattern to decorate the dish, stay with the pattern to become your trademark.

Chef Richard

Sauces

Tahini Dressing

1. Mix lemon juice, garlic, salt and paprika in a Cuisinart or blender.

2. While running slowly add olive oil. At the very end blend in tahini and quickly turn off machine.

Good as a dressing or over vegetables.

1/4 cup Tahini
1/2 cup lemon juice
2 garlic cloves
1/2 tsp. salt
1 cup extra virgin olive oil
1/2 tsp. paprika

Special Ingredients/Tips

Tahini is also known as sesame seeds and can be bought at mediterranean deli.

"Tasty, soft, creamy, delicious, superb, heavenly, ..." are some of the words that people have used to describe the easiest recipe for the dippers. Many people have asked for the recipe to share at parties and in their children's (and spouse's) sandwiches. This secret recipe remains on the party table for only a little while, so make enough for everyone to enjoy and to jar for sandwiches later in the week.

Charles Du Jardin

Herb Mayonnaise

Place all ingredients in a blender and blend for 1 minute.

Makes 1 cup.

1 tbsp. torn basil leaves
1 tbsp. chopped chervil
1 tbsp. chopped tarragon
1 cup mayonnaise

"Love
is a canvas
furnished by nature
and embroidered by imagination."

—Voltaire

Aphrodisiacs

The four S's of love. Succulent, sexy, sensuous strudel! These S's will soon describe you and not the dish. Some cannot place this into a category, but I consider it an aphrodisiac that should entrap any person who is willing, giving, and enrapturing. Take the time to prepare this and plan your evening setting. Include tableware such as dark plates, purple place settings, silverware used for "special" occasions, and silk napkins. The true secret recipe for Escargot should be in the philosophy of the host/hostess and the guest who will be a part of the four S's. I have donated this recipe for you to partake in this experience.

Olga Follette

Zealous Escargot

1. Rub red peppers and garlic with olive oil, salt and pepper. Blacken red peppers and lightly brown garlic in a bowl and wrap with plastic, allow them to "steam" for 10 minutes.

2. Peel charred skin from peppers and puree with garlic in a food processor, set aside for later.

3. Lay out phyllo dough and butter each sheet, cut into 4 squares. Place spinach, goat cheese and escargot on each square (6 on each), wrap and seal with butter.

4. Bake in oven at 400 degrees for 8 minutes.

5. Cut in 1/2 and serve with red pepper puree.

24 pc. escargot
8 oz. goat cheese
12 oz. spinach blanched
5 phyllo dough sheets
4 oz. clarified butter
4 large red peppers
1 tbsp. olive oil
2 bulbs garlic
pinch salt
pinch ground white pepper.

Garduno Family
Milan, Italy

Feeding the body is important, but special attention to nutrients and vitamins for extra energy involved during making love are part of the reason for the magical wonders of this combination of yogurt and sweetness. It originated several hundred years ago (exact time unknown) by the Ancient Greeks as a potent goodness eaten by most of the villagers. When eaten in combination it is considered an aphrodisiac.

Lisa Garduno

Greek Yogurt, Figs and Honey

Mix yogurt with honey and place figs on top.
Decorate with mint leaves or a slice of lemon.

12 ripe figs
12 fl oz. goat's milk yogurt
4 tbsp. honey

Special Ingredients/Tips

Purchase Greek honey for a richer taste. Can be bought at a European Delicatessan.

Angelos Family
Athens, Greece

This is a simple and private recipe. It is shared as an appetizer and aphrodisiac by Hellenic descendants. You may serve taramosalata as a spread over freshly baked bread (from the "furno").

Georgia Angelos

Smoked Salmon and Taramosalata

1. Mix whip cream with taramosalata.

2. Place slicesof salmon on a server plate and spread with taramosalata.

3. Cut cucumber into thin sticks and put a few on each slice of salmon. Season with pepper.

4. Roll salmon slices, and garnish with parsley. Serve with a wedge of lemon.

2 tbsp. whip cream
2 oz. taramosalata
4 slices of smoked salmon
one cucumber
black pepper
1 lemon

Special Ingredients/Tips

Taramosalata can be bought at a European Delicatessan where Greek Foods are sold.

"Give us the luxuries of life and we'll dispense with the necessaries."

—Oliver Wendell Holmes

Breads & Desserts

Von Herrmann Family
Lisle, Illinois

My crumb cake recipe has been handed down through my Grandma whose descent is from Sweden. This recipe has been in her family for decades and I know you'll enjoy its simplicity and richness.

Jill Von Herrmann

Swedish Crumb Cake

1. Mix sugar, flour, baking powder and cut in butter to make crumbs (hold out 1/2 cup crumbs).

2. Add remaining ingredients until smooth and divide into 2 round cake pans. Sprinkle with remaining 1/2 cup of crumbs.

3. Bake at 375 degrees for 20-25 minutes till brown on top.

<u>Make Crumbs</u>
2 cups flour
1 cup sugar
1/2 cup butter

1 tsp. baking powder
1 beaten egg
2/3 cup milk

Special Ingredients/Tips

Add fresh raspberries or blueberries as a topping.

Paris, 1957. After studying alone in Paris for 2 years, the smell of fresh baked bread from the bakery down the block became a familiar scent. Every morning before my classes I would always take it to my apartment, slice it up (still warm) and enjoy the peace and quiet of my home. I enjoyed it so much I decided to begin baking it myself. How hard could it be? I had so much fun trying to come up with original little ideas, but french bread is so versatile. I came up with the idea of baking in some applesauce to give it my own personal sweet flavor. In all actuality you can't even taste it but it does make for a wonderfully moist bread. After trying so hard to change or spice up the recipe, I finally decided that the whole taste I was searching for was the bakery fresh, down home, simple "Old World French Bread".

Tara McClintic

Old World French Bread

Dissolve yeast in warm water with a pinch of sea salt. Set aside. Mix the three dry ingredients - bread flour, baking powder, and sea salt - in a large bowl. For those of you bringing the Old World bread recipe into the New World, follow your bread machine directions. Add butter, applesauce, and activated yeast mixture to your dry mixture. Knead well.

Cover dough with a white linen towel. Let the dough rise in a warm, dark, dry place. Your oven is a perfect place, just be sure your oven is off. Let the dough rise for 20 minutes. Punch down the dough, knead, and cover with the towel. Let the dough rise once again for 20 minutes. This time when you take the dough out, punch it down and roll into two long bread shapes. Place the dough on a silver baking sheet dusted with oatmeal. This is so the dough will not stick, (no buttering or vegetable spray needed). Cover and let the dough rise on the counter for another 20 minutes. Meanwhile, pre-heat oven to 325 degrees. Once the dough has doubled in size, uncover and pop in the oven for 30-35 minutes. Since each oven is different, baking times may vary. You can tell the bread is done when it looks crisp and golden brown on the outside.

1 package yeast
1 pinch sea salt
1 cup warm water
3 cups bread flour
1 large pinch of baking powder
1 teaspoon sea salt
2 tablespoons butter
1/4 cup applesauce
1/8 cup oatmeal

Christmas, 1957. In the heart of a cold winter, my mother put together this palatable pastry that had our tummies hungry and our mouths watering for days thereafter. My mother made this for us during a storm and I have made it for my own family since that time. It contains a tasty cinnamon addition and its smooth flavor lasts for fresh seconds even if they are not eaten soon after baking in the oven.

Sarah Wagnalls

German Puffs

1. Pre-heat oven to 475 degrees.

2. Sift flour, nutmeg and cinnamon together.

3. Cut butter in small pieces and melt slowly in cream.

4. Beat eggs until foamy, stir eggs and flour, gradually, into cream-butter mix.

5. Beat batter until smooth. Fill 6 buttered custard cups two-thirds full, bake 15 minutes, then turn out on a dish and sprinkle with sugar. Serve hot with sauce (or butter and molasses).

Sauce
Combine all ingredients and heat several minutes.

4 tbsp. flour
1/2 tsp. nutmeg
1/4 tsp. cinnamon
1/4 cup butter
1 cup light cream
4 eggs
sugar

Sauce
3/4 cup heavy cream
1/4 cup sweet sherry
2 tbsp. sugar
nutmeg

Novak Family
Aurora, Illinois

There is a tradition for baking this cake, and it still goes on today. Years ago, when my mother was a little girl, her grandmother Anna Mueller, would gather apples from the apple tree in their backyard and bake this apple cake. When I was a little girl , my mother gathered apples from our backyard apple tree to make this cake, and still does today. We have yet to plant an apple tree in our backyard or release this recipe, but I hope to soon (that is plant the tree) to carry on the tradition.

Loree Novak

Family Apple Cake

1. Cream butter and sugar.

2. Beat in egg yolks, then fold in well, beaten egg whites, milk, flour, and baking powder.

3. Pour into a greased square or oblong pan. Place sliced apples close together on top of cake mix. Sprinkle with cinnamon and sugar.

Bake at 350 degrees for 45 minutes.

1/4 cup butter
1 cup sugar
1 tsp. baking powder
2 eggs
1/2 cup milk
1 1/2 cups flour
3 - 4 apples from a favorite apple tree (sliced)
cinnamon
sugar

 Wilson Family
Kenosha, Wisconsin

This special recipe is a lifesaver for mothers and fathers who tuck their children away at night and the children casually say they have to take cookies to school in the morning. This may be a solution. Here's my secret recipe...

Jil Ida Wilson

Forgotten Cookies

1. Pre-heat oven to 350 degrees.

2. Beat until creamy, 2 egg whites

3. Gradually add 2/3 cup sugar
Beat until very stiff (almost 30 minutes or till they hold shape like drawing).

4. Stir gently 1 bag chocolate chips, 1 tsp. vanilla

5. Drop by teaspoonfuls on a foil - lined cookie sheet. Place in oven. Shut oven off immediately and do not open door until morning. You may substitute the various flavors of baking chips but the mini or regular size chips are best.

The beauty of this recipe is that they are practically "bake less".

2 egg whites
2/3 cup sugar
1 bag of chocolate chips
1 tsp. vanilla

Special Ingredients/Tips

For vanilla, try to get Mexican vanilla. Have a friend bring some back from Mexico on their next trip.

"The grand essentials of happiness are:
something to do,
something to love,
and something to hope for."

–Allan K. Chalmers

Unique Beverages

> *Swenson Family*
> *Kansas City, Kansas*

Mother's cold remedy has been taught from several generations of mothers. It is unknown how many generations before, but, I will give my mother credit for easing the discomfort that I had as a child with a cold. The recipe was discovered during the early 1800's while many of the people were beginning to experiment with ingredients that were found in the local store. It has been a helpful aid in lowering the effects of the "common cold". "Used as prescribed" it should help relieve your symptoms or just make you feel warm.

Susan Swenson

Mother's Cold Remedy

1. Blend molasses, butter and ginger in a saucepan and cook 30 minutes over low heat.   Stir frequently.

2. Remove from heat, stir in lemon juice, cover and let stand 5 minutes. Take it warm for best effect in treating a cold.

1 cup molasses
4 tbsp. butter
1/2 tsp. ginger
juice of one fresh lemon.

 Jamison Family
Seattle, Washington

Simply put, this flavorful combination was described by an uncle who had an opportunity to try various cordials during his years as a banker entertaining clients and friends. As he used to say prior to taking a sip, the recipe calls for "patience, understanding, guidance, interest, and discipline...", all the things that a good banker/lender should have. To toast to his delight for preparing this careful and eloquent secret recipe, I have not changed his technique. I hope that you enjoy it as much as many of our guests have in the years past. It has closed several important events for us and I am sure it will add to any business or family gathering.

Tom Jamison

The Banker's Cordial

1. Combine vodka, sugar, honey, almond extract and lemon rind in preserving jar with tight lid.

2. Shake several seconds each day for a month.

3. Let stand 60 days.

4. Strain, then add rosewater and several drops of food coloring to desired color and stir vigorously.

5. Bottle and store. Serve in cordial glasses.

1 pint of vodka
1 cup sugar
1/4 cup honey
2 tbsp. almond extract
grated rind of lemon
4 tbsp. rosewater
red food coloring

Special Ingredients/Tips

Rosewater can be found at specialty food stores.

"You see things and you say 'Why?';
but I dream things that never were
and I say 'Why not?'"

– George Bernard Shaw

Alphabetical List of Contributors

Joseph Akan
Georgia Angelos
Christine Bates
Angie Burdick
Richard Castleberry
Charles Du Jardin
Inocencio Esparza
Olga Follette
Margarita Follio
Lisa Garduno
Tom Jamison
Jeff Klimala
June Kurt
Joan Lesowski
Constantina Linardakis

Nikos Linardakis
Paul Martinez
Tara McClintic
Loree Novak
Antigone Polite
Lee Polite
Rhonda Smith
James Sullivan
Susan Swenson
Jill Von Herrmann
Aldus Von Wolf
Sarah Wagnalls
L. W.
Jil Ada Wilson
Etola Zinni

INDEX

If you wish to be a contributor for future volumes of Recipes Sworn to Secrecy™ please forward your recipe and story with a self-addressed stamped envelope to:

Michaelis Publishing Corp.
2274 South 1300 East
#G8-288
Salt Lake City, UT 84106

Favorite Secret Recipes

_____

_____

_____

_____

_____

_____

_____

_____

_____

_____

_____

_____

Favorite Secret Recipes

Favorite Secret Recipes

Favorite Secret Recipes